WEIRD, TRUE FACTS

The WILD WEST

Brittany Canasi

GOLDMINE

Rourke
Educational Media

rourkeeducationalmedia.com

The United States of America States and Territories in 1884

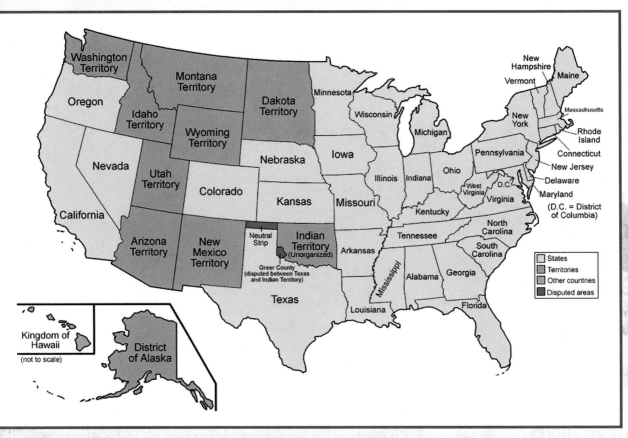

Alaska and Hawaii are the newest states in the union. Alaska became a state in January of 1959, and Hawaii became a state in August of 1959.

Table of Contents

What Made the West Wild

In the mid to late 1800s, the United States was about the size it is today, minus Hawaii and Alaska. But most people still lived in cities close to the Atlantic Ocean on the East Coast. That all changed after the Civil War. Free land and opportunity beckoned families and fortune seekers west. Untamed land stretched in every direction, ready to be farmed or developed.

A Golden Start

The California Gold Rush was the first population boom in the West. Gold was accidentally discovered by a carpenter named James W. Marshall in 1848. Soon after, the prospect of quick riches lured fortune-seekers to the area. Mining camps sprung up everywhere.

In the Wild West, local governments didn't exist. Many settlements were made of land clubs. These were groups of people who settled land before the U.S. government could **survey** the area. They created laws for those who lived there, gave people claims to land, and settled arguments among members. If you didn't follow the laws of the land club, you risked getting kicked out. That was enough to keep order, since being on your own in the Wild West could be risky.

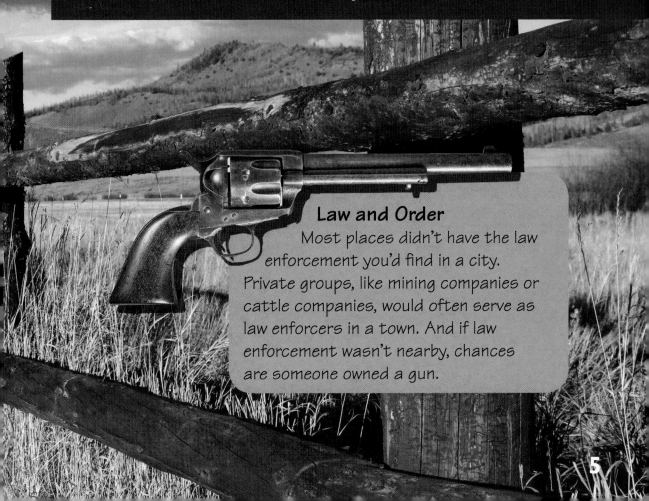

Law and Order

Most places didn't have the law enforcement you'd find in a city. Private groups, like mining companies or cattle companies, would often serve as law enforcers in a town. And if law enforcement wasn't nearby, chances are someone owned a gun.

Howdy, Partner

Cowboys of the Wild West got their cattle herding methods, style, and **lingo** from Mexico. A lot of cowboy words came from Spanish words, such as rodeo, chaps, and buckaroo. Even the word cowboy is a direct translation of the Spanish word for it: vaquero.

Cavalry Turned Cowboy
Many cowboys were former Civil War soldiers from both the Union and the Confederacy. Nearly a quarter of cowboys were freed slaves. The average cowboy made about 25 to 40 dollars a month. That's worth between six hundred and a thousand dollars today.

That's My Cow

Cattle grazed free for most of the year. When it was time to round them up, cowboys could identify their cows by the brand burned into their hide. Every ranch had its own design.

The practice of branding livestock dates back to the ancient Egyptians.

A dozen cowboys would work together to herd about 3,000 cows at a time. They also had a camp cook, a trail boss, and a younger cowboy, called a wrangler, who rounded up extra horses. The camp cook was one of the most important members of the group. Not only did he feed the camp, he was also in charge of finding the North Star each night to ensure the group was traveling in the right direction.

A cowboy's horse and saddle were his most valuable possessions. Some cowboys had their saddles made special just for them. These cost a lot of money! If you were caught stealing another man's horse, you could be sentenced to hang.

Cowboy Lullaby

A stampede of cattle could be extremely dangerous. To keep the cows calm at night, cowboys would take turns singing songs while riding around the herd of cattle. Sometimes a cowboy would sing one line and let his fellow cowboy sing the next, trading back and forth.

Cowboys didn't just dress to look cool. Their clothes protected them. Denim jeans and leather chaps kept their legs safe from rough bushes and branches. A hat with a wide brim was used as protection from the sun. It was also a handy cup when fresh water was nearby! And that bandana around their necks? It was used to shield their mouths and noses from dust.

Cattle Travels
Cowboys would herd cattle about 15 miles (24.14 kilometers) a day. If they traveled farther than that, the cows could lose weight and be too thin to sell.

Cowboys sometimes went weeks without changing their clothes! And they stunk!

Jefferson Davis
(1808–1889)

The last known sighting of a wild camel
was in Texas in 1941.

Did you know there were camels in the Wild West? In 1855, the Secretary of War Jefferson Davis asked Congress for funds to purchase camels for the military to use to haul supplies. By 1857, the Army had imported 75 camels! The herd was split, with some stationed in Texas and some sent to California. Within ten years, the camels that hadn't escaped were all sold at auction. Some were sold to zoos and circuses. By the time the Wild West era began in 1865, the U.S. Camel Corps no longer existed, but some escaped camels still roamed.

Camel sightings in the West sometimes sparked strange tales, such as that of the "Red Ghost." Settlers described a ferocious beast with a terrifying rider on its back. Some witnesses shot at the beast. It got away, but dropped something horrifying as it ran: a human skull. A rancher eventually caught and killed the Red Ghost in his tomato patch. And it wasn't a ghost at all. It was a reddish-furred camel. The terrifying rider was the skeleton of a rider strapped to its back.

The First Inhabitants

At one point, there were 240 American Indian tribes in the United States. They spoke more than 300 languages! As more settlers spread to other parts of the country, the United States government forced American Indians living east of the Mississippi River to relocate to lands west of the river.

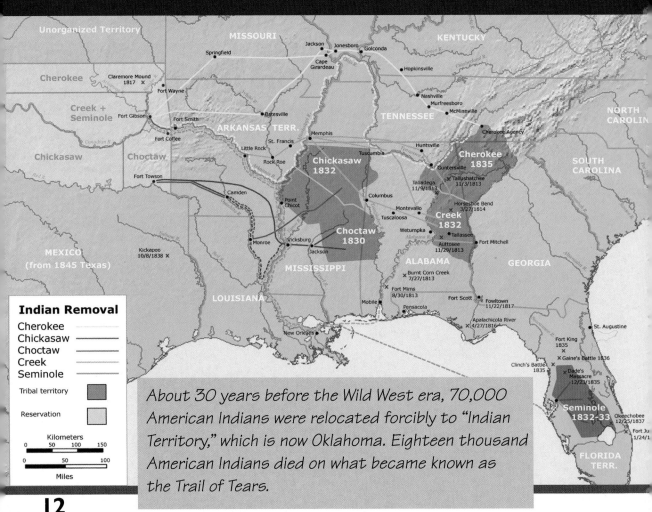

Indian Removal

Cherokee
Chickasaw
Choctaw
Creek
Seminole

Tribal territory

Reservation

Kilometers
0   50   100   150

0   50   100
Miles

About 30 years before the Wild West era, 70,000 American Indians were relocated forcibly to "Indian Territory," which is now Oklahoma. Eighteen thousand American Indians died on what became known as the Trail of Tears.

Famous American Indians

Crazy Horse (c.1840 – 1877) stole his first horse at age 13 and led warriors into battle before he turned 20. When other Lakota tribe leaders fled to Canada, he stayed in the United States to fight until surrendering in 1877. He never allowed anyone to take his picture or paint his portrait while he was alive, because these images were thought to capture the person's soul.

Some researchers think this alleged photo of Crazy Horse is actually a performer from Buffalo Bill's Wild West Show.

When his men surrendered, Chief Joseph said, "Hear me, my chiefs! I am tired. My heart is sick and sad. From where the sun now stands I will fight no more forever."

Chief Joseph (1840 – 1904) was a leader of the Wal-lam-wat-kain band of Nez Percé. He preferred peace to war. He did not think his tribe could defeat the United States military. But when the **federal** government came after Chief Joseph's tribe, he did not back down. The tribe was outnumbered more than two to one, but Chief Joseph led the fight against U.S. forces for months before surrendering. The retreat of Chief Joseph is called the Nez Percé War. It is thought to be one of the most masterful retreats in military history.

Above: Chief Joseph and Family, 1880

Sitting Bull (c.1831 – 1890), a Lakota tribe leader, was asked to give a speech after a railway was completed through his tribe's lands. He spoke in the Lakota language, cursing the people in attendance. The audience didn't speak Lakota, but Sitting Bull paused and smiled during his speech, so they clapped as he cursed them.

Red Cloud once said, "They made us many promises, more than I can remember, but they kept only one: They promised to take our land, and they did."

Chief Red Cloud (1822 – 1909) led a two-year fight for his tribe's lands called Red Cloud's War. He was famous for ambushing soldiers during battle. He would send a few warriors into the open, including Crazy Horse, and lure soldiers in. Once soldiers tried to attack, thousands of warriors would come out of hiding to defeat them.

American Indians fought with the United States government and the military, but they mostly got along with Western settlers. The settlers and American Indians were trade partners, so it wasn't good business to fight with one another.

Helpful Neighbors
American Indians also knew the land much better than some of the newcomers to the West. A settler might even hire a Pawnee or Shoshone guide along the Oregon Trail.

A Shoshone encampment in the Wind River Mountains of Wyoming, 1870.

Sitting Bull with Buffalo Bill Cody

Wild West traveling shows presented fictional accounts of frontier life. Buffalo Bill, whose real name was William Cody, hired American Indians, including Sitting Bull, to perform in his show. This made people think the show was **authentic**. It wasn't. He helped create the **stereotype** of cowboys versus Indians that still exists. The finale of the show usually featured American Indians robbing a family's cabin. Buffalo Bill and his fellow cowboys would rescue the settlers, and the cowboys always won.

Little Sure Shot

Annie Oakley was one of Buffalo Bill's most famous stars. Her nickname was Little Sure Shot. She was such a sure shot that she could shoot a cigar out of someone's mouth.

Stick 'Em Up

Outlaws in the West were as famous as they were infamous. Stories would travel around about dangerous robberies and gunfights, and "Wanted" posters would make their way from town to town in hopes of catching one of them. The reward for catching an outlaw could be as high as 5,000 dollars, which is worth more than 130,000 dollars today.

Jim "Killer Miller" (1861–1909) killed more than 12 people in gunfights. He was also a hired **assassin**. Some called him "Deacon Jim" because he went to church a lot and didn't smoke or drink. He wore a long black coat every day, even if it was hot out. Turns out he hid a steel plate under that coat to protect himself from bullets. It saved his life one day.

Billy the Kid (1851–1881) was a member of the Wild West posse "The Regulators." He killed eight people and escaped jail twice, all by the time he was 21 years old. He never robbed a bank or a train, though. He mostly stole cattle, and every once in a while, a horse. After he was killed, others pretended to be him. This made people think he hadn't really died.

Butch Cassidy and the Wild Bunch

Butch Cassidy

Butch Cassidy (1866–1908) led a posse called the "Wild Bunch." He served 18 months in jail for stealing a horse worth five dollars (about 143 dollars today). When he was released, his posse started robbing banks and trains. They studied the place they planned to rob and stowed supplies and extra horses on their escape routes. Butch fled the country after more than ten years as a wanted man.

Jesse James (1847–1882) led the "James-Younger gang" with his brother, Frank James. Before that, they fought with the Confederates in the Civil War. Their gang robbed trains, **stagecoaches**, and banks around the Midwest. James was killed by a new member of the gang who hoped to collect the five thousand dollar reward for his capture. Many people thought he shared some of his riches with others, like the story of Robin Hood. However, historians have not been able to prove this.

Call the Doctor

Health and **hygiene** standards in the Wild West were much lower than they are today. Many people didn't brush their teeth. Some public eating spots had a single toothbrush made of animal hair that people could borrow if they felt like brushing after a meal.

Beer Beard
Want to wipe beer from your beard while at the bar? You'll have to share the same towel that everyone else is using.

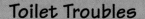

Toilet Troubles

Toilet paper didn't exist in the Wild West. People would use grass, corncobs, bits of newspaper, or whatever else they could find. Indoor plumbing didn't exist either. It was all outhouses or outdoors.

Under-Packed

One guide for people traveling to the West recommended bringing just one extra change of underwear for the three-month journey.

Even the cleanest families usually bathed only once a week. Many people didn't have access to running water in their homes, so they had to take buckets to a well or river to fill a bathtub. The whole family would use the same bathwater. If you wanted to wash up before bath day, you usually had a bowl of water and sponge nearby to rinse off.

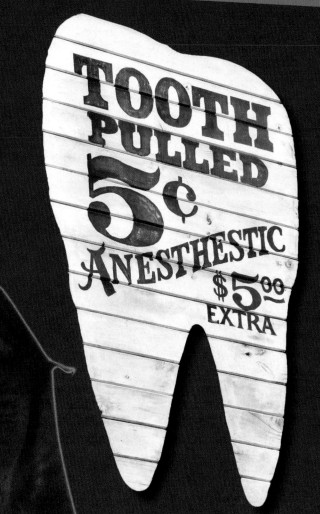

Medical care was not easy to find in the Wild West. Even if a town had a doctor, he probably never went to medical school. Dentists were even more scarce. If you had a cavity, you didn't sit in a comfy chair while a dentist fixed your tooth. You'd wait until the tooth hurt too much to keep in your mouth, and you would find anyone that had a set of tools, like a barber or blacksmith, to pull it out.

Strange Medicine

Some medicines used back then would never be used now. Turpentine was used to help with digestion problems. Today you would use it to thin paint. Guano, or bat poop, was made into a paste and used to treat toothaches. Today, people use guano as a fertilizer.

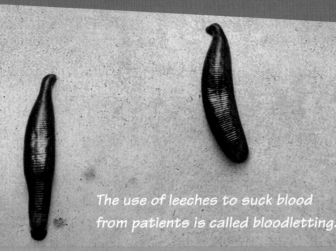

The use of leeches to suck blood from patients is called bloodletting.

Gruesome Cures

Some cures were worse than the diseases themselves.

People used to think that removing some blood from a patient helped them fight diseases. Doctors would attach leeches to a patient, and the leeches would suck their blood.

If you had **gout**, a doctor might kill a dog, stuff it with eggs, nettles, worms, and a long list of other ingredients, then roast it. The smell from the fire was supposed to help you … or so they thought.

One doctor recommended treating malaria by going outside and pouring freezing water on a patient while they were naked. They ended up freezing, and they still had malaria.

Many people died from diseases that we now have vaccines or treatments for, such as cholera, smallpox, tuberculosis, and diphtheria. The average life expectancy for a person was less than 48 years—more than 30 years lower than it is today.

The Silver Screen

Western movies, or Westerns, are usually about a cowboy or gunslinger set in the arid, harsh conditions of the West. The setting of the movie often played just as big a part as the people who acted in it.

Whitewashing

Western movies made the West look like it was nearly all white Americans who lived there. In reality, people came to the West from countries all over the world like China, Sweden, Norway, Germany, Slovakia, and the Ottoman Empire (now Turkey). One Western movie was based on a man named Britt Johnson. Johnson was black in real life, but he was played by John Wayne, a white man. The practice of casting white actors to play these roles is called whitewashing.

John Wayne (1907–1979)

Common plots in Westerns focused on threats to landowners, a lawman bringing order to a town, or a revenge story that involved chasing down a wrongdoer.

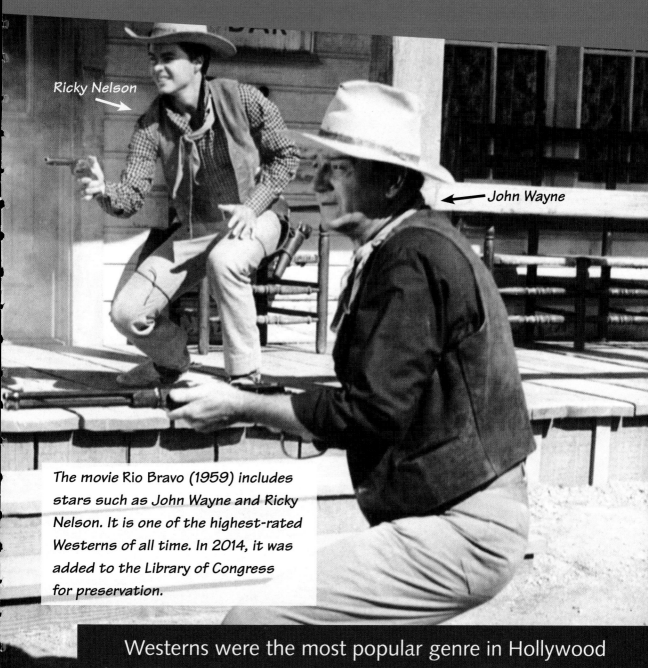

Ricky Nelson

John Wayne

The movie Rio Bravo (1959) includes stars such as John Wayne and Ricky Nelson. It is one of the highest-rated Westerns of all time. In 2014, it was added to the Library of Congress for preservation.

Westerns were the most popular genre in Hollywood from the early 1900s through the 1960s. Many of the movies featured a **duel** or shootout that resolved the movie's plot.

Wild West Myths

Whether repeated as an exaggerated rumor or written in the pages of an old dime novel, stories of the Wild West painted pictures of lawless towns and gun-slinging outlaws. However, day-to-day life wasn't quite so wild.

Myth:

The Wild West was a dangerous place.

Truth: The Wild West was not densely populated, so there was less opportunity for crime. And just because there wasn't typical law enforcement in some settlements didn't mean there was no law enforcement.

Myth:

Guns were everywhere.

Truth: It is true that a lot of people owned guns, but they didn't always carry one around with them. Many towns prohibited guns within their borders. Shootouts were also rare.

Myth:

Bank robberies happened all the time.

Truth: Bank robberies were pretty rare. Banks weren't easy to get in and out of, and buildings were built close together, so getaways were difficult. Historians found about eight major bank robberies over 15 years in the Wild West. To put it in perspective: There were 4,091 bank-related robberies in the U.S. in 2015.

Myth:

Cowboy hats looked like they do today.

Truth: Men, including cowboys, wore all kinds of hats. The most popular hat was actually the bowler hat. Typical cowboy hats looked more like a sombrero, but with a narrower brim and a flattened top.

More Really Weird, True Facts

Many people who moved to the West in search of gold didn't plan to stick around. They wanted to make their riches in mining and return home.

Weather in the West was difficult to bear at times. Parts of the West could reach about 125 degrees Fahrenheit (52 degrees Celsius) in the summer, and other parts could fall as low as minus-40 degrees Fahrenheit (minus-40 degrees Celsius) in the winter.

Baseball was a popular sport in the Wild West. The Cincinnati Red Stockings were America's first professional team. They toured the West in 1869.

Some phrases we think came from the Wild West actually came much later. The phrase "Stick 'em up" didn't appear until the 1900s.

One of the most famous, epic shootouts in the history of the Wild West happened at the O.K. Corral. But in reality, it mainly happened because a group of people wouldn't abide by a town's no-firearm rule. The shootout lasted only about 30 seconds.

There were UFO sightings in the Wild West. In Aurora, Texas, people witnessed cigar-shaped "airships" flying in the sky. One of them crash-landed, and the people who discovered it claimed the pilot was not from Earth.

Glossary

assassin (uh-SAS-sihn): a person who commits murder for money

authentic (aw-THEN-tik): real or genuine

duel (DOO-uhl): a fight between two people using swords or guns, fought according to strict rules

federal (FED-ur-uhl): the central governing body that governs the states

hygiene (HYE-jeen): keeping yourself and the things around you clean, in order to stay healthy

lingo (LEEN-goh): the special vocabulary of a particular group

stagecoaches (STAYJ-kohch-ehs): four-wheeled, horse-drawn coaches used in the past to carry mail and passengers on scheduled trips over regular routes

stereotype (STER-ee-oh-tipe): a widely held but overly simple idea, opinion, or image of a person

survey (sur-VAY): to measure the lines and angles of a piece of land in order to make a map or plan

Index

Show What You Know

1. In what state was the Indian Territory located?
2. Why did so many people move to California starting in 1848?
3. How far on average did cowboys herd cattle in one day?
4. Which outlaw fled the country as a wanted man?
5. What was the most popular style of hat during the Wild West era?

Further Reading

Harris, Irene, *The Homestead Act and Westward Expansion*, Rosen Publishing, 2017.

McNeese, Tim, *American Frontier*, Milliken Publishing Company, 2017.

Stuckey, Rachel, *African Americans in the West*, Rosen Publishing, 2016.

About the Author

Brittany Canasi's job is in cartoons, and her passion is in writing. She has a B.A. in Creative Writing from Florida State University, and she lives in Los Angeles with her husband and very scruffy dogs. A weird, true fact about Brittany is that she would eat cupcakes for every single meal if she could.

Meet The Author!
www.meetREMauthors.com

PHOTO CREDITS: Cover & Title Page ©GaryAlvis, ©kickers, ©duncan1890, ©MoonShot Studios, Pg 13 & 15 ©frentusha, Pg 18, 20, 22, 24, 26, 28 ©Morag Cordiner, Pg 2 ©By User:Golbez, ©Delpixart, Pg 4 ©Stephen Pawlawski, ©bodnarchuk, Pg 5 ©JerryBKeane, Pg 6 ©Glasshouse Images/Alamy Stock Photo, Pg 7 ©Glasshouse Images/Alamy Stock Photo, ©LifeJourneys, ©By beodra, Pg 8 ©abishome, ©CGinspiration, Pg 9 ©John C. H. Grabill, ©CreativeNature_nl, Pg 10 ©wilpunt, ©ZU_09, Pg 11 ©JazzIRT, Pg 12 ©User:Nikater, Pg 13 Unknown_Wiki, ©F. M. Sargent, Pg 14 ©By David F. Barry, Pg 15 ©Arnold, C. D., photographer, Pg 16 ©W. H. Jackson, Pg 17 ©IanDagnall Computing/Alamy Stock Photo, ©Everett Collection Inc/Alamy Stock Photo, Pg 18 ©Ben Wittick, Unknown wikidata:Q4233718, Pg 19 Unknown, wikidata:Q4233718, Pg 20 ©DutchScenery, ©Alter_photo, ©By Tyler Olson, Pg 21 ©By puttography, ©Tetra Images/Alamy Stock Photo, Pg 22 ©Ingenui, ©Craig Dingle, Pg 23 ©sdigital, ©jayfish, Pg 24 ©Walter Oleksy/Alamy Stock Photo, Pg 25 ©INTERFOTO/Alamy Stock Photo, Pg 26 ©KeithBishop, Pg 27 ©Bitter, ©Smitt777, Pg 28 Unknown wikidata:Q4233718, ©milehightraveler, Pg 29 ©MoonShot Studios, ©By Alberto Loyo

Edited by: Keli Sipperley
Cover and interior design by: Kathy Walsh

Library of Congress PCN Data

The Wild West / Brittany Canasi
(Weird, True Facts)
 ISBN 978-1-64516-492-2 (hard cover)
 ISBN 978-1-64516-618-6 (soft cover)
 ISBN 978-1-64516-730-5 (e-Book)
Library of Congress Control Number: 2018930710

Rourke Educational Media
Printed in the United States of America,
North Mankato, Minnesota